Seven
Signs
of
Success

1 2 3 4 5 6 7

THE SECRET'S OUT

By Timothy White, Sr.

Seven Signs of Success © 2016 by Timothy White, Sr.

For information contact:
info@uptownmediaventures.com

Book and Cover design by Tim White Publishing

ISBN: 978-1-68121-106-0

10 9 8 7 6 5 4 3 2 1

Table of Contents

Introduction   **5**

1. The Secret's Out   9
2. What is Success?   13
3. What Does Success Look Like?   17
4. Seeing the Light   23
5. Passion   29
6. Power   33
7. Purpose   37
8. Are We There Yet?   43
9. Be Attentive   49
10. Work Ahead   55

11. Sign 1 Stop   61
12. Sign 2 Caution   65
13. Sign 3 Yield   69
14. Sign 4 Bump   73
15. Sign 5 Wrong Way   79
16. Sign 6 Dead End   83
17. Sign 7 U-Turn   89

18. Are You Ready?   95
19. Get Set   101
20. Go   107
21. Free at Last!   113

Conclusion   **119**
About the Author   **121**

Introduction

The signs are all around us, we can't escape them they're everywhere we look, Hotels, coffee shops, movie theaters, supermarkets, hospitals and the streets are filled with them.

Signs are made for a reason; **they're not for decoration but for direction**. Signs also help keep order, we are accustomed to seeing various signs in our lives, we see them everywhere, they are used for protection, promoting, and encouraging just about everything.

We can't escape them, and many of them influence us in our daily decision-making process. Signs can have physical as well as spiritual meaning, depending on the individual seeing it, and their life personal experiences.

With that in mind, I will be using signs that I believe if seen and understood properly, can lead you to the success you have been dreaming of on any, and every level of life.

There are many signs we see during our everyday travels, but many of them we have become jaded towards, and some we have become almost robotic in our acknowledgment and obedience of them. We see them, and yet we don't, we conform to them, yet don't understand why.

With even the most basic understanding brings power, the power I am referring to is not power over people but power with people, through marketable, and measurable personal success.

What makes success and what leads to failure? Both are found on the same road, and it depends on how the signs are read, and followed, that will produce the difference or desired results.

The signs you find in this book are only seven of literally thousands that we see every day all over the world. Just as signs can help us make it safely from one point to another, they can help us as we move in the direction of becoming successful businessmen and women.

This however can only be achieved if we believe, and follow the signs shown to us faithfully.

Success, however, comes with a price tag, it's not free, and those who seek it must be willing to pay the price to obtain it.

Success is not a joy ride, but it can produce joy. **To be successful you have to go to battle, not against others, but against yourself.**

To be successful there are terms and conditions that will have to be met, and decisions made.

Successful people not only know what to do, but will do it.

Every sign in this book should be paid close attention to, each of them give simple messages or directions that can change your lives.

There are signs that we see all along the way in our lives, as this book will show, that can lead us to success, if we take heed to them and follow the instructions they give us. But, it's more than that, it's not just about what we see, but how it applies and not just what they imply that can help transform our lives.

Success is something you have to prepare for, it's a journey away from one thing, (*or lifestyle*), and to another. Success doesn't just happen, there are tears, sweat, and sometimes even being alone on this journey leading to success.

Success begins with a positive and committed mental attitude; it is the combination of these two operating together that makes for great success.

The road to success teaches us many things if we pay close attention to all the signs along the way, such as the ones I have included in this writing.

If practiced properly and with consistency, we can build a successful life, as well as a successful business, if that is your goal. Are you ready for this journey, I hope so? Now, let's together take a look at the Seven signs of, (*your*) success.

The Secret's Out

Our world and lives are filled with many unknowns, things that are not known to us, or have been kept from our eyes, and ears, some due to fear, and some due to the powers that be, the few who manipulate the masses.

These are individuals working behind the scene who are in control of what we should believe or told to believe. People who move behind the curtains in the shadows who would rather keep the masses in darkness, rather than have them know what they know, and so our lives are filled with secrets.

When something is said to be a secret, it somehow conjures up thoughts it has more value, (*this is what we are taught early in life*), and it's these secrets of the world we strive to know, to unfold, and reveal from God, to aliens and Bigfoot.

But, let it be known that many things we call secrets are in fact not secrets at all.

A secret is something that is known to a few and kept hidden from the multitudes; it's believed to be a truth, or knowledge that is better if not known to everyone.

Well, the secrets out, a once hidden so called

truth will now be revealed to you here, that will surprise many of you, but will change your life forever. Remember what I've already said, a thing that is secret takes on more value and what we will share here is priceless.

There are hundreds of thousands of books in the market, and a large portion of them speak about success, and many of us have purchased them hoping that a secret will be revealed to us that will cause immediate success in our lives (*myself included*), and many of these books have been read with less than positive results accompanying them and there is a reason for this.

Motivational books are like weight loss programs. There are people who say the one they follow is best and works because they had results, but how can that be, so do they all work? Those who use various ones say yes. Here's the simple reason for that, all of them work, and yet none of them work, impossible you say? Think about it. They work only because the individuals not only believed they would work, but applied themselves to assure that it did.

Books, self-help, dieting, or whatever book it is, don't change people, this only occurs when the reader makes a conscious adjustment, and addresses themselves honestly about who they are, will they change their personal reality.

This might surprise you, but there is NO SECRET TO SUCCESS. But as this book suggest there are signs of success.

One of the keys to success is to stop looking for some secret formula to achieve it; the signs have been all around us as well as in us, but many of us have been programmed (*and self-programmed*) to believe there was, and is **some secret backdoor** that leads to it.

Secrets have a common thread within them, they are not completely factual, and it is a presumptuous altered view of the truth for the purpose of control.

Secrets, because they are labeled such, we are quick to assume they are true because we did not have knowledge of them.

Many of these "secrets" once we know or learn of them, we realize they should never have been considered a secret in the first place, because knowing "the secret" added nothing to our lives.

So, the secret to success is that there is no secret to success, there are revealed things that if we put them into practice will lead us to the success that we seek.

This book will only point you in a direction, and hopefully help you see the world of possibilities that are already inside you, that only needs a jump start, a charge, and a little mental push to get you moving.

The so-called secret is out, and the success you seek is not hidden somewhere that you can't find or obtain it. We have been taught to look everywhere for success but inside ourselves. The key to your success is, and has always been YOU; this book will simply show you some of the signs to look for and apply as you move in the direction of fulfilling your dream of success.

W. Clement Stone said, "if you believe it you can achieve it", and in the book Everything I know at the top I learned on the Bottom by Dexter Yager he said, "success is the realization of a worthwhile dream". Both are very true statements, but only if they are believed and applied in our lives.

What is Success?

How success is defined, will vary from individual too individual, in large part this is due to what that individuals understanding of it to be, or have been told it is.

Everyone believes they know what success is, at least according to them. Of course, this does not mean they are wrong or right in their definition; everyone defines success based on their system of beliefs or experiences.

For example, we are told that success is financial accumulation, that the more money you have the more successful you are, and that "**money is king**", (*or queen*), and that "**money is power**". The more money, the more power and this makes us successful.

Others see success as being able to afford that million-dollar home or taking extended trips, without worrying about when they have to be back at work.

Maybe success is driving that car you always wanted or having a different one to drive every day of the week. Could these things be the symbols of success?

Let's go off the beaten track for a moment, to

see how still others define success.

There are some who see success as something as simple as completing a test, and getting an A, graduating from high school or college, or finishing a race they entered. There are some who have married and say in spite of their differences, and the ups and downs in their relationship, their marriage is a success, as it has stood and endured the test of time.

There is a very simple definition of success that I would like to give, and it does not require Webster Dictionary to define it.

Success is the accomplishment of one's goal, its triumph over something or over self; it could be over drinking, smoking, swearing, or any number of bad habits or an attitude.

Success is achievement, personal and/or financial, but here's the one I love most, that I use to define it, SUCCESS IS VICTORY!

To gain victory (success) one must have **personal involvement in planned actions** as we will discuss in the following chapters.

Victory, or success comes as the result of overcoming resistance, obstacles, and objections, not in others (*that comes later*) but in you.

Successful people succeed because they are

unwavering in their commitment to pursuit their goal. As we have said, the so-called secret is out.

You will determine what path to follow; Success is making a conscious personal choice which direction you will take in your life.

Try this for a moment, replace the word success with the word victory or victorious as you continue to read this book, and **not discover, but uncover** the power that is found in you by doing so.

What Does Success Look Like?

This is a troubling question for many of us, because we are asked to make success something we see as tangible, to give it a physical description. Some people see it as the abundance of material things.

The more we have, the more we are seen and classified as being successful.

Wealth is the measurement of success to many of us; this is due to the brainwashing by media that having such "things", is the status quo; you are seen as nobody until you are surrounded by often expensive things.

Success, we have been programmed to believe, is to live in exclusive communities and drink expensive wines and flying around the world in a personal jet. But the truth is, having these things and the ability to do them does not equate to success.

I heard someone who was wealthy say, this is exactly what someone who is poor would say, someone who has nothing.

Success does not mean striving to be wealthy, wealth might come as a byproduct of success, but it is not what success is or what it looks like.

It's far easier to see what wealth looks like than it is to see what success looks like, as people think they are one in the same, but not so.

Wealth is material, where success is mental and spiritual in nature. Many lives are being destroyed because they believe they have to have things, expensive things to be considered successful, but wealth accumulation is not success. Material things can become a trap to those who are deceived by them.

Am I saying material things are bad, or that it's evil to have them, absolutely not, what I am saying is material things should not be the major goal in life.

We live in a material world, so it's not possible to ignore material things, but many of us are living for them, and believe this to be the true measure of success.

Life is about balance. Is it possible to have wealth and be successful as well, yes, and is it possible to be successful without wealth? Again, the answer is yes. Here's the balance, and what success looks like; it's having the PROPER MENTAL ATTITUDE.

When we think of success, we think of things acquired, not things accomplished. For example, there was a man in the 1968 Olympics, and his name was **John Stephen Akhwari**.

Many people don't know who he is, or what he did. He was a marathon runner in that year's summer Olympic, his story is a remarkable and encouraging one.

He was from Tanzania it is the largest country in East Africa, bordered by Kenya and Uganda to the north; Rwanda, Burundi, and the Democratic Republic of the Congo to the west, and Zambia, Malawi, and Mozambique to the south.

John Stephens story is simple; he was sent by his country as one of the delegates representing Tanzania for the marathon in Mexico City. He entered the race with 75 other runners but during the grueling run 18 people dropped out, finding it too much for them to take.

But as they ran, John Stephen was bumped, and fell to the ground injuring his knee and shoulder, the air was not what he was used to in his country, there were now two reasons to pull up and quit like others, but he was steadfast.

Akhwari was encouraged to drop out from the race, but there was something inside him, driving him onward, so he continued even being in personal and physical pain.

Here's the remarkable thing, all the remaining 56 runners had completed the race, the crowds had become thin, and the closing ceremonies was taking place, and awards were being given out for the winning runners.

John, had been all but forgotten at this time, the first place runner (Mamo Wolde of Ethiopia) had finished his run with the time of 2:20:26. Akhwari finished well over an hour later with a time of 3:25:27, not only last, but dead last.

What is it that sets this story apart, it was **John's persistence**, he refused to quit, and he refuse to give in or give up?

Everything seemed to be against him, but there was a hunger, a power, and a determination that drove him to continue, and make it to the finish line.

Why in spite of the things he suffered would he continue when he knew he was last, and would receive no reward, or glory for his effort?

When asked why, he responded, "my country did not send me thousands of miles to start the race, my country sent me thousands of miles to finish the race".

This race for John wasn't about winning or even competing; **it was about finishing what he had started.**

Success (or victory) was not about what John Stephen Akhwari would do, but rather what he would complete.

Success is about completion, not competition, again we say success is not about money it's a mentality. What does success look like? It's steady and constant movement forward towards a personal goal or objective, its overcoming fears by faith, and it's seeing beyond where we are, to where we want to be, and moving in the direction of fulfillment.

What does success look like; take a look in the nearest mirror, and you will find a success story waiting to be told.

What will be your success story?

Seeing the Light

The journey you are on will require you to see things in a different light, (*no pun intended*), to open your inner spiritual eye, to see what has been there all along.

Seeing the light, a simple statement that carries with it great authority. If you are to be successful, you must prepare yourself for it.

Everything in life is about preparation before product, it's that defining moment that sets you apart from others (*I didn't say makes you better than others*).

Seeing the light is an acknowledgment, of 1) that it's there, and it was placed by someone else, and 2) that it serves a purpose. You also have purpose.

YOU ARE UNIQUE, and one of a kind, you must start with this truth, knowing this however means very little if you don't BELIEVE AND EMBRACE IT!

We like lights, were created by The Master Designer and placed here also to serve a purpose.

As we move forward, you must embrace this positive mentality or everything you do will be lined, dipped in, and covered by fear, and failure.

There are a few word statements you need to remove from your vocabulary that have been taught by others as a way of life, but can cause your downfall.

For instance, how often have you heard people (*or yourself*) say "I can't do that"? This statement has detoured many of us from what we have been created to be and do.

This statement is one of defeat, not action. The speaker, (*if it's you*), has already conceded to a new action even before an attempt is made.

"I CAN'T", denotes personal involvement and action, it is the assumed belief that whatever is being asked cannot be done by that individual, and this without even endeavoring to see the possibilities.

"I'LL TRY", another of those phrases that should be destroyed. I'll try has a built-in excuse, for an action not taken.

What do we mean when we say I'll try? We are telling the individual(s) not to rely on us to complete our given task. I'll try is laced with an unwillingness to comply.

"I MIGHT", it is the cousin to "I'll try", it is saying basically the same thing but with a dash of hopeful doubt.

I might come through later on, the end result is the same as "I'll try", when nothing is done, and there is no follow through.

I think you get the picture, to see the light means to change how we think (*internally*) and what we do (*externally*).

The road to success begins with a self -check list, what you say to yourself, and what you believe about yourself, will determine how successful you are or will become.

Preparation is the first step you have to be willing to make, or better yet, watch what you say. It's about SELF TALK, and it's about what you say to yourself, before saying it to others.

Prepare your mind by watching, and monitoring what comes out of your mouth.

If you believe negative things, you will speak negative things, the mind controls the mouth, not the other way around.

Seeing the light is to be illuminated, and it is to acknowledge the need to change. Change what you believe, change what you think, change what you've been doing, and change where you are heading.

Now let's look closely at the light ahead of

you. It's time to start making decisions, and choosing a direction.

The light you see will only burn as bright as you allow it to shine.

This book is about learning to be aware of the things that you can do once you make certain needed changes to your life.

Even though there is no color in the pictures our minds let us know what color goes where, and the location on the traffic light.

We will be speaking about each of these lights in descending order, and what they mean in this book and possibly in your lives.

You've seen the light, now let's explore it together, and see where it takes us on this, your road to success.

Your success begins as you reverse or backward plan. This means, looking at the potential things that led you to the place you are now, and where you will be next.

Consider the following moving forward. There is a much bigger picture here that we should concentrate on; it's a visual lesson that can teach us many things spiritually, if examined and studied carefully.

The journey we are on requires us to see things that once seemed to be hidden from us, but once we change how we view them, the things we didn't see unfold to us, and we begin to see them very clearly.

Passion

Red light

Passion, what is it, where does it come from, and who has it? As you can see, I have it located on the traffic   signal that is red in color, and there is a purpose for this, as we will be speaking of very shortly

But first, what is passion, some synonyms are, ache, desire, hunger, craving, urge, fervor, zeal, a powerful intense emotion, these are but a few.

It is defined as a very strong feeling about a person or thing, an intense emotion, in Greek the verb is, υποφέρουν (*to suffer*).

As we move forward, it's important that you see yourself as your own best example. It's always easier to see others in the light we seek to shine, and see their problems, but rarely are we willing to stand in the light ourselves.

If we are to be successful, then we must see ourselves for what we truly are, and the way we truly are.

Success does not come from making excuses or finger pointing, success is internal producing external results. The success we are speaking of begins with passion, and it comes from a willingness to suffer for what one believes in, even dying for that belief, if called upon to do so.

Stop right there, did I say die, you say you have passion, but it has its limits, you say you believe in what you are doing, but dying is taking it a bit too far.

For many of us, passion is a word that sounds good, and makes the user appear in some eyes, to care about what it is they are doing, they make all the right noises, and say all the right words, but their passion is hollow.

It's a band wagon passion, it's a going along for the ride mentality, and it's crowd pleasing. In other words, there is a false passion, a passion that is driven by profit only, and self-satisfaction.

There is also a lustful passion, it is not about helping others, but has an agenda that is self-indulging and selfish. So, as we talk about passion, stop and evaluate where you are taking it, or is it taking you?

Our passion excites us, and it can stir us to take action. For example, if your passion is singing, it keeps you excited about singing, if it's teaching, you can't wait to teach, if it's writing you eat, sleep, and breath to write and share what you have written, to share what you have learned, or to share the music you have written.

Having passion is not enough, it's like having a car with no engine, it's talked about but it's not going anywhere.

Can you teach people to have passion, not really, it's already built into each of us, it simply has to be triggered and released, and by triggered, I mean discovered or acknowledged.

What will it take to trigger your passion; I can't answer that for you, but maybe before the end of this book, you will know and understand yours?

All human beings have been given a talent or talents by God that is to be shared with the world, but is having passion enough?

Power
Caution

Everything in life is powered by something; it has an external or internal power source. Power is a source of illumination and strength; it can be an internal control driven by your already mentioned passion.

Notice if you will, the placement of power, it's on the caution light. With power there is always a caution as it could be used negatively or positively, this will depend on the individual who has it.

As with anything, power, influence, authority, or control, can be abused. Consider this, in a traffic situation when we come upon a caution light, we usually have to make a quick decision concerning it, do we race to make it through it, or slow down, stop, and wait for it to change.

Caution means, always being vigilant or watchful, as we have seen many accidents take place because of someone being in a hurry to take the light before it changes.

Being cautious, is also to be careful, to be watchful and observant, even mindful of what could happen. It's being proactively minded. In other words, it's a control force put into practice.

So, you are Passionate, motivated and excited but then what?

You need some juice, some power to get going.

What happens when you come across a stop light that is not working, it has no direct power as it is cut off from its source. You can't ignore it, but, you have to adjust how you treat it?

The light has a presence, but no power. The light poses no real danger that comes from those who don't respond properly to it. Notice where we have placed the power.

Power is on the caution light, Power, (*authority, rule*), is good, but how it's used can make or break you as you travel towards your success.

In traffic, the caution light means it might be possible to make it through the intersection before it changes, but at what cost to you or others? You can speed up, and race through it, but in doing so you might bring about something you were not expecting, or you might come to a sudden stop that could similarly bring about a chain reaction of events not considered. Power, the energy of forward momentum must be used with caution.

Power is good, if used with restraint. Each of us has been given the ability to power up your passion, and once we do, once we understand the power inside us, accompanied with caution, it will be impossible to remain where we once were, and why is that?

Power comes from being connected to a source of energy which gives purpose to our internal power.

You have the vehicle; the engine, (*the power source*) is in it, but what now. For some reason the car still sits idle, and why is that?

What good is power if it is not understood, turned on, or used?

Passion can get people excited, but it needs to have power also, and what good is power, if it is never recognized for what it can do. Power here is located on the caution light for a good reason. Many of us don't know how to use power properly. Power is not bullying others to show you have it.

Power should be used carefully, and cautiously, not carelessly. Humility should always accompany power, it's not something to show off, but share. If you are to be successful, you must be cautious with the power you have been entrusted with.

How is power to be used? Passion and power are strong, once they are combined with one more ingredient.

Purpose
Green light

Each of us were designed, created, and born with a purpose, but it's up to us to learn what that purpose is, and practice it.

There are some general signs we can look for as we develop mentally and emotionally, that can help us as we travel through our lives on this planet.

Our lives were no accident that happened, as some might want us to believe, and our purpose, (*thou unknown by some*), is to do more than eat, drink, be merry and die. And it certainly is not to be self-centered, self-serving, or selfish.

Our purpose is to make positive change in this world and to leave it better than when we were introduced to it; this is done by learned knowledge, or early experience.

Have you discovered your purpose, what you

were designed and created to do? Most people are going through life miserable and unhappy, because they are not doing what they were designed to do, but rather what others have told them they should do.

The purpose driven life is a life that is constantly being transformed and renewed DAILY.

You have noticed where I have placed purpose, it's third in order on the stop light, (*by descending order*). This was not done because it is less in the order it was placed, but rather only as a reference marker for the individual to see.

In fact, you can arrange them any way you choose to, but all of them must apply, if you are going to be successful in life.

Purpose is located on the green light, and the reason for this is clear, PURPOSE DRIVES YOU.

Purpose helps define who we are, and who we will become; **purpose helps us move in the direction of accomplishment**. Purpose is the fuel that moves us. Passion is the car; power is the engine, but these don't matter if there is no gas.

I've spoken to numerous individuals over the years who have told me they had no purpose in life, or didn't know what their purpose might be. Some of us would think this is unusual, but it is more common than not.

Understand this, we are being bombarded with information overload both positive and negative all the time, 365 days of the year, do this or that, become this or that, these sources audio and visually are all around us, influencing us on every level, ever so slightly and subliminally.

We are taught usually by family members to do or acquire certain life skills, trades or jobs, that **"they feel"** we are best qualified for. Or jobs that we are ethically more suited to. One career more than another (*Asians, Technology, India, Doctors, Blacks, Sports, etc.*), and in due course some will be successful if they just follow what they were told would be best for them.

There are more than a few who have taken the family's chosen path, and found they were happy and fulfilled. This was not because their parents chose or defined their career or purpose, but, that that individual was placed on the correct path early in their life internally, and was able to see it, and act on their designed purpose for themselves.

Purpose is defined as intent, the reason why something exists, is done, made or used.

We often apply this thinking to material things produced and not human beings, but each of us, as we have already said, has a purpose. It's discovering the reason why we exist, and why we do or don't do particular things.

How many times have you asked a child what they wanted to be when they grow up only to find they were not limited in their imagination, but if their answer was not the one family chose or hoped for them, the family would do their best to convince them to change that career path?

What's our purpose for being in this world, our reason for being alive, what will be your story and what will be your legacy?

We begin with our passion, we understand our power, and finally develop our purpose. These three are fundamental, as we begin to build our lives around them.

Each of us has a purpose, but we must pause and reflect on what that is, or if we are passionately with power, pursuing it. And if we are not sure, there are ways to learn what it is.

We are never too old to change, or too young to follow our dreams. Don't be blinded by those who would say it's too late, or that you will change your mind many times as you get older.

Success, like understanding, has no age or limit to when it can become a reality in our lives. Some successes come later in life, some earlier.

Discovering one's purpose breathes new life into them, it adds value, and a sense of worth and fulfillment.

Purpose, answers several why questions, why was I born, why am I here, and why am I doing this thing?

Purpose fuels our reason for why we do what we do, it green lights our passions power. To understand our purpose in life is to help change it.

Purpose thrives in the person that is passionate, and the person who understands its power. Purpose has been given the green light; it's time to get moving.

Are We There Yet?

The words generally associated with a child coming from the back seat of the car asking that age old question, "are we there yet?"

What's the purpose of this question being asked? It's asked because of restlessness, and boredom, because it seems to be taking far too long to get to the place expected, usually Disney World, or Sea World or some other place of entertainment and pleasure.

There are those of us who even after seeing the light (*of reason*), do not accept its power or authority in our lives, most times due to pride and arrogance, not being reachable or teachable.

Hurrying can cause for undue delays, success is building consistently, not hurriedly.

When we hear this question, are we there yet? It conjures up a picture of impatience, and anticipation by the one speaking them.

The child anxiously looks forward to the journey, but not the time it might take to get them there.

Success is thought of much in the same way by those who seek it, they want and desire to have success and as they embark on the journey towards it, some quickly become impatient when it does not take place as quickly as they had hoped or planned.

Just as the child seeks the reward of their participating in the journey of just going along, they feel this is more than enough for them to be rewarded, even if they put little to no thought or action into the end result. For them, success should be theirs because they are along for the ride.

Are we there yet, requires no effort on the speaker's part, they contribute nothing to the trip, they are simply a passenger, often not paying attention to the signs along the way, had they been doing so, they would have known how far they were from reaching their destination.

Restless, impatient, annoyed, frustrated, and discouragement, all begin to fill the mind of the individual who is not in the place of control, THE DRIVERS SEAT.

Complaints are all byproducts of a hurried individual who believes others are in their way.

Instant gratification, it's asking, "what or why is it taking so long"? This question is frequently asked by someone who is contributing nothing to the completion of the journey.

Those backseat manipulators, and adjudicators, have no interest in what it takes to get from point A to point B; they just want to get there as quick as possible, and to know, why is it taking so long?

Never mind what it will take or the cost to get to your desire destination, they offer only complaints.

Being successful is limiting and putting the brakes on those who are giving nothing and doing nothing but going along for the ride from distracting or sabotaging your plans. Although they complain and whine, they are also useful to a small degree. It is their chronic negativity that can also be the source of power and push to complete the task before you. It's the itch that needed to be scratched and sometimes poked.

On the path to your success you must be willing to let those who are simply going along, family, (*spouse, children*), and friends, (*although it's wise not to have them along in the first place*), to remain silent, and enjoy the free ride they have been given.

This does not mean they don't have anything to offer, but, it should not be in the form of distractions, complaints and confusion.

Does that sound harsh, only to those who are guilty of doing it? There are people who are going nowhere in their existence, and doing nothing with their lives, and yet will spend time trying to tell you what to do, and how to do it.

Are "WE" there yet, the question is asked as if that individual is making things happen, they are including themselves as a contributor by asking ARE WE THERE YET?

Successful people wisely choose the company they keep; they keep association with like-minded individuals, dream builders not dream killers. This is also a sign although not visual. So, what will it take moving forward to reach the point that you feel or believe you are successful?

That's the reason you are holding and reading this book, it is to help you redefine or reacquaint yourself with who you truly are inside and out, and begin to make the necessary adjustments to change your life for the better. It's understanding why you do what you do, so please continue. You are in the car, in the back seat of knowledge, learning how to get to the front seat of understanding, and moving carefully forward with wisdom to arrive at SUCCESS.

No, we are not there yet, but we're getting closer.

Be Attentive

Keep your eyes opened, watch where you are going, and be alert. Each of these is a call to action.

Being attentive, is paying attention to the things that surround you, but not getting caught up by them, or entrapped by them.

Everything in our lives is here for our use; they are guides to help us make our success a reality.

Success is an idea whose time is come, and is brought to reality by faithful diligence, and commitment. As you sit in the back seat of opportunity, you are to be attentive to the things you are about to see and hear.

Your success requires "you", it's calling out to you, you have been chosen and given an assignment, a talent, or a gift to share with the world, and it begins here, it is to 1) LOOK, 2) LISTEN, 3) LEARN, and to 4) LIVE, by application.

There are successful people, and there are as many people who have the ability to become successful, and have not, and the major difference between the two is that successful people will take risk in order to achieve their goals in life. Whereas, those who want to be successful often become their own worst enemy, by not taking any chances, only venturing out so far, but will remain close to whatever excuse they can adapt to, so as not to take any risk, for **fear of failure.**

Seeing all the right signs mean nothing if you never take the appropriate follow up action.

We all hear those small voices in our heads telling us or suggesting to us what to do.

YOU will only do what you choose to do, no matter what the voices in your head (mind), says to you, this is called CHOICE.

Successful people have rules, and morals they follow as they journey through life, even taking negative experiences and turning them into positive actions. Are you attentive, time to find out?

LOOK.

This is to be observant, to have a watchful eye, its connection by way of visual stimuli. It's using our inner spirit eye; everything we do is done on the spiritual level, and brought into the real or physical world because we live in a physical world.

Remember we can't see thoughts, or ideas until they are translated into tangible computations, or pictures that others can see to acknowledge.

See the established, you can't change what you don't see, (*or refuse to see*), the fruits that exist and understand, is that anything can be improved upon. Look inside yourself and hear the voice that tells you to "let go", and that "you can do it", see the possibilities that is you.

Look at where you are coming from, where you have been and then where it is you want to go.

LISTEN.

There are people who have done something similar to what you might be thinking about doing, spend time with them, get a book that has been written by them, and read. Having ears, but unwilling to use them for the purpose they were created, will slow any progress you make.

Listening is a forgotten skill, and sense we are flooded on all sides with information overload, it becomes harder to discern what's good advice, and what's bad advice, but it can be done.

Listening is done with the intent to learn, to make one better. Listening stabilizes and balances, it means I don't know everything, and being willing to sit and absorb all we can, and it means, making adjustments. And carefully adding steps in our success progress. Being attentive is listening.

LEARN.

Now that you are listening the next question is, have you been learning anything? The drawback to learning is not applying what we learn.

There are individuals who have been seated in the midst of knowledge, and wisdom daily, (*if they are attentive*), yet, have learned nothing more than how to misuse what they have been exposed to, and merely project an appearance of knowledge, yet no changes can be seen in their lives that suggest they have learned anything.

The challenge is not in what we think we know, but rather what we are willing to learn.

LIVE.

It all comes down to this, once the earlier mentioned, look, listen, and learn are applied, a new life can begin.

Successful people are attentive, they are watchers, they are listeners, they are learners, and certainly live, and are lively in the things they do and even in the company they keep.

You are the company you keep, if anyone wants to know who you really are all they have to do is look at the people you are associated with, you are known by the company you keep, not the justifications you make for it.

By the way, the voice I spoke about, that speaks inside us is called conscious, and it was given to us at creation for the purpose of helping ourselves and others.

Work Ahead

There are people that were born who did not have to work hard for anything in life, as they are given everything on a proverbial silver platter, and there are those of us who have to put in the blood, sweat, and tears, to accomplish many of the same goals in life.

This would seem to be unfair, if we look at it the wrong way. What do I mean by this? If we are busy focusing on what others have, or how they might have obtained it, then we lose sight of what it is that we are doing, or what we can accomplish in our own lives.

Many of us would like to take the easy road to success, the road that has no bumps or ditches to avoid. The road we would choose would be paved with gold and diamonds, but is this the road to true success?

The road you and I are about to travel is not a road that is paved in such a manner, in fact, it will have everything many of us would rather detour around, if given the option to do so.

The greatest success stories have come from those who have traveled the hard roads of life. Your challenge is to make a choice at this point, and that's whether or not you are WILLING to proceed. There will be much work ahead, if you decide to continue going forward.

This is a sample sign to look at, one like others that could easily be overlooked. But it's important as you begin this road trip on your path to success.

This sign reads simply "Work ahead". Remember what we've already said, success comes with a price tag, and if you are not willing to work to achieve your success, then ignore this sign, turn around and quit now, before you get started.

You can't continually move forward while looking backwards.

Success means you have to get out of Park mentally and emotionally, and into drive. Revving the engine will not get you where you need to be either, a loud engine does not mean fast or reliable, and while it will get you noticed, it will not get you where you want or need to be.

"Work ahead", means you can no longer stall, put off, or hope someone else will do the job for you. IF IT'S YOUR DREAM, YOU BUILD IT.

It would be a great disservice to you, if someone else did all the work (*and there are those who see this as success*), but then why should others share with you when they have done all the work?

Successful people know they have to get a little dirty while working and building their dream. I want you to know that it's not hard work, but its consistent work, and that, ultimately pays great dividends.

Recognizing the work ahead leads us to the prize we seek. Once you have made up your mind to take this simple leap of faith, you must factor in this, "do you really believe you can do this"?

Many have said yes, to this question, but there is another question that must be asked that is more important than the first one and it is, **"Will you finish what you've started"?** Many have started out on the road that leads to success, but somewhere along the way they stopped, turned around, and quit.

There's a simple reason for this; **they were not ready or willing to put in the work required** or the time it would take to complete the task before them.

If your dream is road worthy, then there will be work ahead, if you are going to see it come to life.

You can't build a business or be successful in any endeavor by doing the things you have done in the past, those are the very things that kept you bound. **It's impossible to achieve what you don't believe,** so, you can't begin this journey with doubt.

By the way, old acquaintances and friends can be a stumbling block in preventing, or at least slowing down your success. How so, simple, they don't believe in or endorse you, or what you are doing.

And of course, there are those old habits and ways, we cling to and justify our holding onto them, and yet we wonder why we are not moving forward.

If the people in your circle ARE NOT ACTIVE workers, doers, and contributors, why are they in it? Success is the result of clear focus, combined with passion, as we will discuss shortly.

When you have a vision of what you believe can change the lives of others, or your own life, you have to be willing to do the work necessary to make it a reality, which is part of the reason why this book was written and titled the Seven Signs of Success.

Well it's time to get started, so buckle up.

STOP

Sign 1

Before you go any further or make another move, you need to consider what it is you truly want to do, what you are willing to let go of, and if this is a journey you are committed to take.

It will take commitment on your part, and a clear vision of what you intend to do.

Success is not something that just happens, it's chosen, and even if most people desire it, it's often unattainable and the reason for this is clear, the work that it takes is unwisely ignored when the signs are all around.

Sign 1, a stop sign is your first introduction that can lead to your success.

The stop sign is not for pausing, it means what it says, STOP. Evaluate where you are before you make your next move, the decision you make will be one that will either take you to your dream, or prevent you from obtaining it, so please consider the following carefully.

Stop, does not mean as many of us are used to, what is called a rolling stop, which is nothing more than a pause and not a stop, and it's considered illegal. We should not try to make or take shortcuts to our success, we, you, must be willing to go the distance as success means different things to different people as we will show, as you continue.

There are a few things you need to know and do if you are to be successful.

Stop making excuses and start making changes. Everything you do will depend on your mindset; your external actions which are influenced by your internal desire.

Stop sitting around planning and not producing. It's very easy to sit around and to talk about what you want to do or going to do, but that never gets the job done. In fact, the more you sit and talk about doing anything, often what you have found is you have done nothing but made excuses not to begin, or to begin and not complete a task.

Stop blaming others for your lack of motivation. It's not anyone else fault that you are lazy or complacent. Yes, I said lazy, it's one of the major killers of success.

Stop listening to others who are going nowhere. If you're sitting and listening to those who are going nowhere, you have gone nowhere yourself, and although it may seem they have talked you out of pursuing your goal in life, it's you, and you along who puts the final stamp of rejection to your dream(s).

Stop planting yourself in front of the TV when there is work to be done.

You can't plan a successful life around your favorite program. The time to enjoy them (*if you feel you must*), is when you have accomplished what you have set out to do. Make that show (*for many of you it's your sports fix*), if you want to watch it, make it a reward for the work you have completed, and not left undone.

Stop signs are placed in front of us to remind us to come to a complete halt, see where we are, and see if we are moving in the direction we wanted to go.

A stop sign does not mean stay where you are, it does however remind us to examine where we are, before we make our next move. **It's a time of immediate reflection and choosing a direction**.

A rolling stop shows lack of obedience, we are not careful of what could happen, or the consequences of our actions should we be pulled over by the police, and because of our negative actions we seek to blame the police for doing their job, or someone or something else (*maybe running late to the job, interview, or TV show airing*).

What is the first requirement on the road to success, STOP?

When you leave a Stop sign you have to be careful, and cautious as to what you will do next.

Caution

Sign 2

What is caution, and what does it mean? It's sign number 2, in our signs of success. It means be careful, to give thought to what you will do, it's moving with assurance and not randomly, or with confusion.

There are Caution signs in business as well as life, that we must take note of; we encounter them that they may help us be ever mindful that where we are going could pose possible or potential hazards, and danger along the way.

Caution signs let us know there's something ahead that can lead to harm if we lose focus or take our eyes away from the objective or ignore its warning.

Caution signs, remind us that someone has been where we are going before us, and there is possible danger awaiting us.

Caution doesn't mean going from zero to sixty, it means moving away carefully and deliberately.

Successful people pay strict attention to the signs around them. **Caution does not mean being fearful**, you don't turn and go the other way because of things that could possibly take place on your life's road that you don't understand.

A caution sign, like all the signs we will be covering, are teachers of the road, that let us know what's to come, and that whatever is ahead is manageable, even though having a potential for harm.

Some of us panic when things don't go as we had planned, and in doing so, it stalls our success, even if only for a moment.

A caution sign reminds us to be watchful, not quit.

If you have no life ambition, there can be no business ambition, our lives are reflective of our dreams, hopes and aspirations.

If we don't believe we can be more than we are, our lives reflect that, and others will see it as well. The old adage, that says, "ACTIONS SPEAK LOUDER THAN WORDS" is true.

Being cautious is good, but being fearful of what might happen without even venturing to see what could take place, is foolishness, caution does not mean stopping, it simply means precede forward but being careful as you do, caution does not mean with speed.

Successful people are cautious not fearful.

Caution means examining carefully as you proceed, cautious people are not speeders, and neither are successful people. Successful people don't hurry along, and are not rushed; they take their time, and manage their time wisely. When you can understand the things that can possibly go wrong, and respond to them in advance, that's being proactive not reactive.

Be careful to observe, read, and follow life's instruction, and directions given by the signs you see, they can be warnings or direction that can change your life and even save it, if applied properly and timely.

Yield

Sign 3

There's more in the world than we can imagine or think. Another sign of success, sign 3. We have to learn how to Yield or give way to others.

To yield is to humble ourselves in order to see things better, if not from a completely new viewpoint.

Successful people learn from others, and successful businesses learn from other businesses what works, and what does not work.

Yielding does not mean stopping, but rather evaluating while proceeding forward.

Yielding is sharpening focus. It's listening and not always talking. It's watching and carefully observing while in motion.

Yielding is not weakness, it's a form of wisdom. To yield is to place one's self in a strategic position to get into the flow of things without incidence or interference.

Some might see this as compromising when it is not. Compromising is when two or more people come to an agreement concerning specific matters only agreeing because they do not have total control of the situation or circumstance.

Successful people know **when to yield**, as well as **how to yield**. Yielding is having the patience to wait for the right moment to move forward, and not just rush into things.

Successful people know they don't have control over everything that happens in their lives, and even the most successful people have to be willing to slow down, and reflect on where they are, and how they can become better.

A person who is unwilling to yield is someone who will most certainly be in or will be the cause of an accident, it could be business, personal, or financial.

Success that is enduring is tempered by patience. Be careful of the people around you that are telling you what they think as there are many individuals going nowhere and will do what they can to prevent you from being successful, they are usually people who have been around for a while, and who can become backseat drivers, **you might**

hear what they are saying, but be mindful of what they are doing and contributing in your life as you seek to fulfill your dreams.

Yielding is not giving up but simply giving way, it's allowing another the immediate right of way.

Success is not only about what you see but how you respond not react.

Responding is guided even anticipated movement through temporary and necessary compliance.

The road to success is filled with decision upon decisions that will help you hone your skills and talents, but bear in mind it's up to you how each of them will be applied in your life as you move in the direction of self-fulfillment.

Yield, it's taking a deep breath, as you continue with your forward movement of entering into the flow of the traffic of life. It's slowing down just enough to decide how you will proceed forward. Yielding is a time of decisive evaluation while on the move heading in the direction of your desired destination.

Bump

Sign 4

Successful people, and those who are sincerely seeking success, realize they wil be met with obstacles along the way, those unforeseen bumps that will have to be addressed, that if not addressed, can cause additional problems along the way.

The bumps we hit on the road of life can become the **bumps that we allow to block the way to our success**.

Succesful individuals will use bumps in their lives as building blocks.

Bumps in the life of an individual seeking success, is not something that makes them afraid, but it instead opens their eyes of internal creativity, it teaches them how to turn a lemon into lemonade.

We can hit bumps at unexpected times, and they are often seen too late to avoid, and we hit one or two along the way.

Bumps can inflict major harm in only a few moments. There are bumps we can get around, and there are bumps we have to deal with. Successful people learn to deal with bumps. Some bumps are the people we refuse to disassociate from, they are people we know mean us no good, but we don't let them go, and they keep you from growing.

The bumps in the life of anyone who is committed to following their dreams can vary, bumps are unexpected negative distractions. One of the greatest pitfalls to becoming successful is distractions.

Distractions (*whether people or things*) **pull and tug at us** to render us useless if we begin to focus on the damage the bump potentially caused.

Bumps are small and yet there are those who make bumps into mountains in their lives and sabotage their own hopes of becoming successful.

Bumps are minor inconveniences, and can be annoying, but they should never deter anyone from success.

What are the inconveniences one might ask? It depends on the dreamer. You have to ask yourself, what is it that you have allowed to be part of your life that YOU are using as an excuse to not follow your dream.

What is the primary source of the bumps in your life, now be honest, what, or who came to mind? If you're not willing to face the truth, you will only continue to do what you have done, which has kept you from the success that has been calling out to you for some time.

A bump can be large or small but no matter the size, can cause major damage if not dealt with; a small bump can throw a car out of alignment, making it hard to control a vehicle, and can lead to injury of self and others.

This sign, and the ones to follow, can help prevent those little things in our lives from causing major problems, by simply paying close attention to what you are doing, saying and believing.

Some bumps are hidden beneath other obstacles, and are not immediately seen, such as advice (*usually bad*), that was never asked for from individuals who believe they know what's best for you, even when you can clearly see by their lives they are going nowhere.

It's wise to consider the source, before acting on advice they give.

Because an individual is close to you, does not mean they know what's best for you, or even what your plans or goals are.

Bumps are like bad advice, they are everywhere, they cannot be avoided, but they do not have to disable us.

Some bumps are more severe than others, but they put us in a place of mental change and development, and they can be very irritating but can always be overcome.

There are the bumps of criticism, bumps of arrogance, bumps of pride as well as bumps of jealousy, and of course, bumps of defeat.

Each of these can serve a positive purpose, once we acknowledge why they have been placed in our lives. And here's the key, they were brought into our lives not to weaken us, but to MAKE US STRONGER.

What is the lesson that you have gained from the bumps you have faced over the years? Did the bumps in your life cause you to complain, or change things?

Understand this also, we are all part of the problems that surface or part of life's solutions. So, I ask you now, how have you been handling the bumps in your life?

Wrong Way

Sign 5

Have you ever taken a wrong turn while you were driving? Often this occurs because we lose focus, are tired, or become distracted.

Every once in a while, on the journey to success, we might find we have made a mistake or two.

Some of the greatest errors we make, come from thinking we can do things on our own, that we don't need help because we already know where we are going, and we know what we are doing. Nothing could be further from the truth.

Success is collaboration, its inclusion not exclusion, and there's nothing worse than discovering you have taken a wrong road, (*emotionally or even psychologically*), or to have made some bad business decisions because of being ill-equipped, and pride would not let you admit you were wrong.

Don't let your ego have you continue down a wrong path. When all you have to do is ask, or simply take a different direction. There are very few people successful or otherwise, who have not made a wrong turn here or there in their lifetime. But going the wrong way is not as bad as continuing down that road, believing it's okay, and that "things", will work themselves out. Having the wrong mentality will keep you going in the wrong direction.

Successful people will always admit when they are wrong, or when they have done wrong, why? Because during the course of the argument they're aware time has been lost, and the possibility of lives and opportunities being lost can result from continued delay.

This 5th sign, the wrong way sign makes you aware that someone else has done what you have done, and that there's nothing wrong with accepting this fact, and doing what is needed to make it right, before harming others or even yourself.

Going the wrong way and seeing the sign quickly enough, lets one know they might have time to get turned around, if it is done quick enough.

The wrong way sign is a warning that you are not traveling in the right direction. **The acknowledgment of a wrong, is a key to being successful**.

A bad decision emotionally or financially, can have dire consequences, and affects in our lives, if not acted on immediately. The wrong choices made in our lives is often based on emotions, and not intellect, and how we feel, rather than what we know.

Going the wrong way for successful people is not listening to others, who in spite of the signs posted (*given*), will tell you that it's okay to remain where you are, just move quickly and you will be fine. The chances that others will take and the mistakes they have made should never become yours. **The danger comes from hearing and not paying attention**. This brings us to another sign of successful people.

Many people have lost their lives because they thought they could take a wrong path, and things would somehow work themselves out in their best interest.

Stubborn people will take the wrong way, and say they know what they are doing, or it's their life let them live it. The wrong way sign lets us know that continuing on that path only leads to trouble, if not adhered to.

Making a wrong turn and going down the wrong road happens to even the best of us, there's no time to feel guilty, or have pity parties, just do the right thing, TURN AROUND IMMEDIATELY.

The immediacy of danger and harm makes us act quickly if warranted. If you are to be successful, the only thing you should do quickly is change your mind about how you will continue to operate.

The wrong way sign lets us know immediate action must be taken to avoid possible injury.

Distractions and loss of focus are two of the many ways we can find ourselves going the wrong way in our lives, and business relationships.

This book is not about me telling you what to release in your life, but things you should avoid. As you continue to read, it will become more apparent what you need to do, but for many of us this wrong way is the best time to blame others for where we find ourselves. Remember what we said in the earlier chapter BE ATTENTIVE; the signs are the keys to your success.

Dead End

Sign 6

This sign says it all, there is nowhere left to go; this is the end of the road. This sign sadly is seen, embraced and accepted by many people. It's the quitter's sign.

Where whiners are welcome, where fear becomes fact, and throwing in the towel or raising the white flag is acceptable. This sign does not mean that there's absolutely nothing to be found there. Just that it's time to decide what to do next.

There are many people living on the dead-end street of their minds. It's those who have had their dreams diminished, and hopes dashed, (*often blaming others*). This sign is posted on the road that often leads to personal anger, resentment, and assumed helplessness.

This is the sign that tells those who are not willing to make change, to **come and settle down here you've done all you can do**.

Dead end is the place to go and **give up,** rather than **get up, even being surrounded by the signs of success.**

Let's take a closer look at this dead end. What's it really all about? For many of us, we live what we consider a dead-end life, working a dead-end job, surrounded by people with dead end conversations and lifestyles.

Many of us also have dead end friends, and remain in dead end relationships, and the reason for this might surprise some of you. It's because, "they", YOU, have a dead-end mentality.

The sign dead end, is the work that is associated with the mentality of the person living there.

A dead-end mentality is one filled with panic, resentment, blame and misery. A dead-end mentality is not a healthy one, nor does it lead to positive reforms in one's life.

Dead end streets are to be avoided at all cost, unless of course you live on one.

To advance in life, we must remain on the open road, be opened minded, and we must have a positive mental attitude as we move forward. All the signs of success point in one direction, they all point upward, and forward.

I mentioned several types of dead ends; we need to examine them to see how they can affect our pending success.

Dead end life. A life that is said to be going nowhere, one that is stuck in a rut, a life that has not changed in years. It's going the same places, eating the same foods, driving the same car, even wearing the same clothes, this is a life STUCK IN THE PAST. This is a life that is filled with complacency and not diversity.

For some individuals they have settled for a dead-end job. They don't believe they can have or even do better, because they don't think they have the qualifications that others have, that would make them suited for certain positions in life.

They, (*by way of friends and family*), have been told they would never amount to anything, or that trying to move up in a company is useless, they are out of their league.

Employers need workers, not thinkers, not people who understand they can by more than an employee.

Many of us are not happy in the jobs we have, because we know in our hearts that we are more than just an employee. But have settled to be just that. And to make matters worse, we have family and friends who tell us that, this is all we can be, and should not strive to have or be more than, "THEY", THINK WE SHOULD BE.

A dead-end mentality is debilitating, it can cause us to remain dead inside emotionally, mentally and spiritually.

For your further consideration, the sign dead end, also let's some of us know, that we are in dead end relationships, and these relationships often become our excuse for not leaving the dead-end streets of life.

At the heart of dead end, is FEAR. Many of us fear failure so much that we willingly do nothing to change our lives, and rather blame others for our being stuck on dead end streets. Every sign we have seen, requires a decision to be made, and you as the driver is the one who has to make it. You, and you alone. Your life's success is based on the things you will do. There is hope for all of us, if we are willing to take the next step; this is that pivotal moment, so let's look at the 7th and final sign.

Consider this, as we are about to take a look at our final sign. There are people who willingly take dead end roads, they are people who shun responsibility, they seek the shelter of complacency, and as unbelievable as this might sound, they run from success, and settle on the dead end road of life.

U Turn

Sign 7

When should someone make a U-turn? Aren't they illegal? Some are, but not all. And since we are talking about success, these signs are all to be taken spiritually and not physically. These and all signs were designed to bring about certain actions. **Every sign you have seen in this book, and will see in your lifetime, is a call to action.**

And as we come to this the last of the seven signs of success, our thought process should now be challenged to change. It's time to do an about face, a reality check, an evaluation of self.

Honestly, these signs have only pointed you in the direction of success, (*if applied*), but THEY CANNOT MAKE YOU WHAT YOU DON'T WANT TO BECOME.

So when and how, should someone make a U-turn? it should be done safely the moment one realizes they have made a wrong turn.

Wrong thinking can lead to negative actions, (*wrong turns*), putting us on a destructive path that calls for us to make a U turn.

Taking the wrong path can come from lack of preparation, not paying attention, lack of concentration, lack of sleep, and assuming things without knowledge or facts.

Yes, in some places a U turn is not legal, but in life it's always good to make a U-turn, to turn a life around. It's better to make that turn (*when it's safe to do so*) than to ruin or take a life.

A U turn, turning around and going back, this does not mean going back to the beginning but going back to the point where the confusion began, going back to get a better and clearer look at what happened to bring about this error. It's better to make a U-turn than to continue down the wrong path. A U-turn comes from personal introspective of self, and not examining someone else.

Successful people examine themselves carefully and daily, even the mistakes they make. This is done in the hope of not making the same mistake again, and learning from what they did wrong, and to do it right.

What is it in your life that you are willing to keep with you, even when you know it's not benefiting you in the pursuit of your goals?

Is there something you are trying to make fit, and work when you know it does not belong?

With the advent of the GPS (*Global Positioning System*) we are subject to make fewer mistakes, but we will still make them, and where there are human beings involved, there will always be mistakes made.

Sometimes we have to revisit where we were, to clearly understand where we're going. A U turn is a sign that lets us know we have to go back and see what we did wrong and correct it. A U-turn is seeing the mistake you have made but with urgency change it.

Successfully minded people move with a sense of URGENCY and purpose, they know they cannot recover the time they have lost due to their mistake, for not paying attention, but they can make a difference from the moment they became aware of what was done, if immediate action is taken.

The need to make a U-turn shows a temporary loss of direction and time, but it does not mean a goal has been lost; it is only a minor glitch that has become a training tool for the future.

Successful people are not afraid to take risk, risk that's clearly seen in the signs of success.

A U-turn is an important sign and I listed it last for a reason. There are two things you notice when it comes to the U-turn. First, it's in the shape of a "U" and second it requires YOU, the individual to personally make it.

The U-turn is not a dead end; it takes us away from the thing(s) that could become problematic if we continue on that particular path that could stall us, or even cause some of us to give up and quit.

The U-turn gives us an opportunity to see where we went wrong, and to go back and get our bearings, to clear our minds, and continue forward towards our goal.

If you have noticed I used the term "Successful people" any number of times throughout this book and for a good reason.

They are individuals who do not lose focus even when their faith seems to waver; they understand what they seek is bigger than their faults and fears.

Success is not a word that is spoken, but actions that are taken; it's clearly seeing an objective and making it a reality.

So, I ask now, have you seen the 7 signs of success?

Well there are just a few more things you need to do at this point they are in the next few **bonus chapters**.

If you are going to be successful, you must also mentally apply these three simple steps. Don't look for the finish line, just enjoy the lessons the journey will teach.

Are You Ready?

Your success has been guaranteed, but will depend on what you are willing to do and whether or not you follow the instructions you have been shown.

Now that you've been given this simple formula that can lead you to your success, are you ready and willing to follow and apply it?

If the answer to this question is yes, then you are reading the right book at the right time.

You've seen the signs, there was no magic wand waved, or crystal ball used to predict your future success and outcome.

Your success will completely, and totally depend on what you will do now that you have reached this point.

I have spoken of **Seven** *simple* **signs of success**. The human mind always seeks simplicity (*even as we complicate these matters*), the brain always seeks the best, and often the most convenient way to get things done, even that which is said to be impossible, but will require work.

Through the years that has changed, and we began to over think, and overdo things, in large part because difficult is profitable, and the longer a thing takes to get done, the more money there is to be made (*sorry, but the secrets out*).

Inspiration, preparation, and dedication, three basic requirements needed as you move in the direction of your success.

There are a few questions you need to ask yourself as you get ready to move forward.

First, are you serious about what you propose to do?

Second, is there a time frame you have to reach completion?

Third, how will your success influence others?

Fourth, what are you waiting for?

Have you been inspired by an event, a thought or even a vision to step out of the shadows and leave your footprints in the sands of life? There is no better time than now to act. What is inspiration without preparation, no true measure of success is obtained without them.

Many people fail to become successful because they put stumbling blocks in their own paths, remember the questions you have asked, they mean nothing, if they are riddled with doubts and fear. The questions no matter how good they are, mean nothing if they are words only.

Getting ready means realigning things (*or removing people*) that slow you down or will hold you back, success doesn't just happen, YOU HAVE TO PREPARE FOR IT.

Preparation begins with honest self-evaluation, a personal mental inventory; this is an important factor as we move forward.

In this genesis of your success, I have asked if you are serious, and many will say they are, but they lack commitment, they have a fire in their heart, or as we already detailed have a passion but, it grew dim almost as quickly as it started, and one of the reasons for this is what I like to call **subconscious sabotage**.

What is that you ask, it's the power behind all physical, and mental action, it's what we have told ourselves, and believed to be true. It is the act before the action.

Bear in mind this thought, there is no one that has the ability to make us quit, give in, or give up, this is done from the inside out, there is no one that can talk us out of doing anything but us, we simply strive to find people who will say what we want to hear and believe, to agree with what we chose subconsciously to believe was true all alone.

Getting ready means to prepare your mind first, if you truly believe it, you will achieve it.

The second thing I spoke of is framing, what is the framework or time you have imagine for the completion of this particular task. This becomes a guideline for your successful endeavor, this does not mean you have failed if you do not meet this date of completion, what's important is that you have made tremendous strides towards your goals which in itself is deemed a success.

As you continue to move forward remember, this is not a matter of competition but completion, we put far too much stress and strain on ourselves because we have been brainwashed into thinking everything we do is a competition to show we are better than someone else.

If we are to compete, let it be against time, not to finish first, but to finish right. You are at the starting line, but as you look around, (*which should not dominate your time*), you see you are the only one there, it's not how fast you are or even what number you are, your success is determined by your completion, not where you finish. Stop competing and focus on completing the thing you have started.

I asked a third question and that was how will what you do influence or affect others? Success is not a solo act, and although it involves us personally, the results can be seen, locally as well as globally depending on what we do. This does not mean our focus should be on pleasing people, or what they think about what we are doing, but having an understanding that what we do can have a significant impact in the lives of others.

Fourth, we will speak on more in the next chapter, once we have everything in place then there is no reason to delay, no longer time to put off, it's time to break the chains of our subconscious fears, and act.

Get Set

What good is it to suit up, if you really have no desire to get in the game, and what good is it to build a system, if you have no plans to use it? So, why dream dreams if you have no intentions of fulfilling them?

We have dreams, and visions that they be fulfilled, that they can change a life or change the world. We have been designed and created with a purpose, not just to mull around or simply sit around. Each of us are here to help make life better for the next person, and generation. To get set, is to position ones-self for that purpose, and for what is to come next.

What we do now, will always affect what we will do next. Getting set, means to get in place, to prepare, but getting in place is something we have to willingly do.

I went to a track event for my granddaughter, and I watched many children competing against one another, because they are being taught that life is about winning, that everything is about competition, and coming in, and being first.

But I don't think many noticed that day, that the individual who ran in the first lane, did not finish in first place.

Life is not about where people will place you; it's about where you see, and place yourself in relationship to life.

Life, is about your personal mentality, it's about if you are ready to face it, and where you have placed yourself. For each sign we see in life, there is the need to get set or prepare for what will follow.

Getting set is internal, we have everything ready, so we think, and planned out to the last detail. But what does that matter if we never act on it, what good is it to prepare for something then not follow through with it.

It's like planning a vacation to the Islands, buying the tickets, packing your bags, getting to the airport, and then changing your mind for fear.

This fear I speak of is not something that transpired at the airport, it was there all along the way, it is better known by another name, DOUBT.

Getting set means we have to remove or challenge the things that can cause us to remain stationary. What do I mean, why sit in the car revving the engine making a lot of noise when you know you have no intention of driving the vehicle, the vehicle is ready to go? It's set in the right position, and sounds good, but when it's time to move, the driver stalls. There is nothing wrong with the car, and for the moment let's call the car success.

The car (*Success*) is ready but the person in charge of it falters and stalls before they take the final steps to achieving their goal.

Success is having everything in place and moving forward, it's not about winning it's about willingness.

How long have you been waiting for the green light in your life? Have you heard the horn blowing in back of you, and a voice telling you the light is in your favor? It's just a reminder to get moving, and that you have set still long enough?

Getting set means reviewing, it's the last check stop, before going forward, it's a time to reflect on why you are there, as well as how you got there. Getting set is where everything will either come together, or fall apart. No move is minor, they are all major.

Get set, is being in the right place, and the right time with the right mentality. It's having, and generating internal excitement, and anticipating the next move to come, not with fear but with focus. Getting set is having all things in order, it's seeing them in proper perspective, and being prepared to move immediately.

What good is this, if the motivating factor is now missing, a once positive mental attitude becomes cloudy, and doubt sets in?

Some success is negated by those who don't believe they deserve it. They FEEL it's wrong for them to enjoy better things, or have a better quality of life. Once you are set, you have to be ready to LET GO.

Let go of what? Everything that is a needless weight in your thought life, your subconscious must change from negative too positive, and your, "CAN'T" must become "CAN".

Remove the **"I'm in it to win it"** mentality, and see it as **"I'm in it to finish it"** mentality instead. It doesn't matter what place others see you in, or where they might seek to place you. You win by completion not by competition, you are successful by simply staying the course, and seeing it through to its end, whatever that might be.

Getting set does not mean, being set in our ways, but rather getting set to move from old ways, with swiftness, looking, and being ready to move forward positively.

Go!

Go, time to move, time to get going, time to put into practice what you say you believe and have learned, it's time to make your success live and thrive.

All things have come to this point in time for your life, to see if what you say is true. Your success begins, and ends with what YOU will do, not what you say moving forward.

Words are numerous but actions give power and life to our words. Go means nothing, if you are not willing to do so.

As human beings we are taught to believe success is about accumulation of things, or how many expensive toys we have, this is material gain, but this does not equate to, or mean success.

True success is achieving personal goals that have been set and met. It's going the distance, or seeing things through to the end, again this is not about winning but finishing what you have started.

Go, does not mean fast, but it does mean steady, to have a pace, it also means being able to project an end time, based on specific movement. Successful people are forward thinkers, even futurist, seeing the unseen, and believing it to already be possible.

Go, to quickly relinquish a once occupied space, to leave behind. Go is a word the demands an action response, and a sense of urgency. Success, though it does not happen quickly it does require mobile consistency.

There are things we must do, and things we must willingly leave behind if we are to be successful, but understand this, going forward, does not mean abandoning.

There's a teaching that if you are to be successful you have to abandon family and friends, in order for this to take place, this is not altogether true as abandon means to leave completely, to utterly forsake, to desert.

Where there are some who spout this as the way to success it is not true, but those on the other side of the fence if you will, that are waiting to see quick results of success often feel as if this is true, that they have been abandoned, not so much physically but emotionally.

As the saying goes," if it were easy everyone would be doing it". To focus on a dream and to pursuit it, is not going to be easy, or acceptable to those who demand of your time.

For those who do not or cannot see your dream, to them you are simply wasting not just your time, but theirs as well. Their belief is, that they should be the center of your attention, so in order to move forward towards your success, you have to make an internal decision to abandon old thoughts and actions.

To abandon something, is to change directions mentally before it can take place physically, and in this case, it is NEGATIVE THINKING.

Go means, LETTING GO, getting off the breaks and placing your foot on the gas petal, to stop revving the engine of complacency, it's putting your thoughts into drive, and going forward positively.

Success is something you have to prepare for, and believe it or not, there are as many who are afraid of success, as those who are afraid of failure.

Many are called, few will respond, so what does that mean? It means no matter how much the individual knows, sees or understands, they will not do what they know can and should be done, because of fear of what will happen should they become successful. As strange as that might seem, there are those who have great talent and abilities, but will do no more than recognize that they have abilities, even being told by others they should use them?

Yet these same people, do nothing more than once in a while show a glimpse of their abilities, and making excuses, as to why they cannot go forward.

It's like having the ability to build a great car, one unlike anything on the road, showing it off, and yet never driving it, being afraid something might happen to it. Success is not just knowing what you know, but sharing it with others.

Henry Ford did not become a successful businessman because he had a great idea for transportation, but, rather because he acted on it, making his vision of a car a reality.

So, now what are you waiting for? Haven't you been paying attention to the signs, and moving forward, or are you just in the way impeding traffic. Don't you hear the horns of life blowing, telling you it's time to get going?

If you're not willing to go, just pull over, and get out the way. There are people trying to go places, are you going places, or just in the way? Who or what are you allowing in your life to block and keep you from your success?

Will this book simply become a tabletop book, and dust collector, or did it give you some insight into the person you can become, and your own success story?

Free at Last!

Freedom is not free; it took work on someone's behalf to achieve it. It is an offer to be emancipated, to be released from a former captivity. There are many of us who have been led to believe we are free, but if that were true, then we would be at liberty to do what we want, when we want, and as long as we want.

Everything in life comes with its own attachments, they might not be so obvious, because they are taught to us from the moment we are born, and from generation to generation, until we graduate mentally to accept them as true. History has been demonstrating to us that if a cycle, a doctrine, (*teaching*), or thinking is not broken, it will be repeated time and time again, and from generation to generation.

Many of us don't realize we have been enslaved to believe certain things, and that others are programming us, and controlling what we see, hear, and do.

Others, whoever they are, if they can control us, then there is no fear of us. These same individuals, once they see anyone attempting to gain their freedom become fearful.

What does this mean, "they", see the self-awareness taking place, the mental freedom that is changing the individual's life, and they see someone who has become self-aware, and no longer have to be poverty's puppet? This self-awareness or freedom opens the eyes and changes the road that is thereafter traveled.

Freedom clears the view and distortions of the mind, and it sees the personal possibilities as a now liberated individual.

How does one break these chains after being oppressed for so long? One of the keys is to develop new thought habits, to change the way you think about yourself, and become action oriented.

Once you know something is wrong, the time to act is immediately, being aware means nothing if we simply wait on someone else to act on our behalf.

Your dreams have been given to you, that you give them birth, and not keep them locked away in your mind.

As we have already said, success is victory, it's overcoming personal objections, and obstacles that have been place in front of you, or inside you by others.

Information can bring with it, knowledge, and knowledge transforms lives, not just any life, but yours personally. Understand the truth, and the truth will make you free, spiritually, mentally, emotionally and financially.

This choice to change, is yours and yours alone. You have to be willing to give up that slave 9 to 5 mentality. You have to be willing to remove the excuses you have been making over the course of your lifetime, and the he, she, "they won't let me" excuses.

What am I saying? EXCUSES ENSLAVES US, and you will never be truly successful making excuses for why you are not successful.

Life is filled with hurdles to overcome, and if you fall, you simply need to get up, and not blame the thing you fell over, but continue to run.

Once our minds have been liberated, we can honestly, and sincerely choose the best direction to take our lives. And the success we have longed for and dreamed of, will be ours.

There are a few statements or phrases we often use concerning ourselves that help keep us from our SUCCESS FREEDOM, each containing only four words such as these...

I don't have time

I'll think about it

When I get time

I need more time

I'm too busy now

It's not my fault

And, talk to me later

These and other words used, like "I'll try", "I might", and "I'll see", all are connected to failure to complete a task.

Freedom does not come from the words that others say to us, or about us, but rather, the words we speak to ourselves about ourselves.

Stop being a slave to your negative mentality, your faultfinding, and your finger pointing. I can't get ahead because of so and so. Success is freedom from mental manipulation, which is driven by internal and unnecessary personal fears and insecurities.

Free at last, free at last!

Conclusion

Now that you have seen the signs, what will you do, will you continue to make excuses or make changes? The path to success can't be made any clearer. You can never be the same with the knowledge you have now gained, but it's possible to remain where you are, if you are not passionate, or understand the power that's in you, and you listen to those around you, or the voices inside you, that tells you that you can't do it, you can't, or won't be successful.

All things are possible when you believe. This book is nothing but words, if you are not willing to apply the things it says into your life. It's like medicine, what good is it if prescribed, but you never take it, your success is in your hands.

Your freedom is in your care, to have and enjoy completely. The signs of success are all around you, but more importantly they are inside you as well.

About the Author

Timothy White Sr. has impacted thousands of people throughout the world as an author, teacher, motivational speaker and minister. Mr. White is on a mission to positively influence millions of people through his work, ministry and writing, which currently exceeds 80+ books covering a plethora of topics including bullying, domestic violence, self-help, history and spirituality.

The Cleveland, Ohio native, a father of five, has overcome many adversities in his life including homelessness and losing his beloved wife to cancer in 1994. Through much heartache and disappointments he discovered a new purpose and passion to use writing as a tool to "plant positive seeds."

Mr. White has developed profound spiritual insight into relationships over the years. Mr. White has written multiple books on the topic of abuse including, *In the Ring with Heels On, She's the Boss and Victims of Bullies*. Mr. White writes about these and other issues because of the relevance, and prevalence of domestic and other violence. He believes that, **"Information plus application equals transformation."**

Mr. White is an Evangelist and former pastor. He believes, "God chooses who He uses." He writes, speaks, and ministers to local, national, and international audiences. With an additional 15 new books in the works, Mr. White hopes to give people plenty of "spiritual food" to eat.

White is one of the producers of the documentary ***"Where's Gina?"*** about missing children on which he was also narrator.

He is a co-developer of a tech company (Gsys LLC) that brought blindside technology to vehicles that made billions for the industry, saving countless lives. He is currently co-hosting a radio show, ***"Healing the Hurt"*** on WERE 1490am in Cleveland, Ohio on Thursday evenings 8-10 pm with Host, Rev. Brenda Ware-Abrams.

He is currently on the Advisory Board and is a volunteer instructor at the Juvenile Correction centers in Warrensville Heights and Cleveland, Ohio where his book *Seven Signs of Success* is being taught. His book *Victims of Bullies* is, currently, in the City of Cleveland School system to help stop and make aware of solutions to the issue of bullying.

timwhite55@gmail.com   Timwhitepublishing.com

Made in USA - Kendallville, IN
1199377_9781681211060
11 24 2020 1303